Does the Richness of the Few Benefit Us All?

Does the Richness of the Few Benefit Us All?

Zygmunt Bauman

polity

First published in 2013 by Polity Press

Polity Press
65 Bridge Street
Cambridge CB2 1UR, UK

Polity Press
350 Main Street
Malden, MA 02148, USA

ISBN-13: 978-0-7456-7108-6
ISBN-13: 978-0-7456-7109-3(pb)

A catalogue record for this book is available from the British Library.
Typeset in 12.5 on 15 pt Adobe Garamond
by Toppan Best-set Premedia Limited
Printed and bound in Great Britain by Clays Ltd, St Ives PLC

For further information on Polity, visit our website: www.politybooks.com

Contents

For the man who has will be given more, till he has enough to spare; And the man who has not will forfeit even what he has.

(Matthew 13.12)

Wherever there is great property, there is great inequality. For one very rich man, there must be at least five hundred poor.

(Adam Smith)

This disposition to admire, and almost to worship, the rich and the powerful, and to despise, or, at least, to neglect persons of poor and mean condition is the great and most universal cause of the corruption of our moral sentiments.

(Adam Smith)

    do not banish reason
For inequality; but let your reason serve
To make the truth appear where it seems hid
And hide the false seems true.

(Shakespeare, *Measure for Measure*)

Introduction

A recent study by the World Institute for Development Economics Research at the United Nations University reports that the richest 1 per cent of adults owned 40 per cent of global assets in the year 2000, and that the richest 10 per cent of adults accounted for 85 per cent of the total wealth of the world. The bottom half of the world's adult population owned 1 per cent of global wealth.[1] This, though, is only a snapshot of an ongoing process. Even more bad news for human equality, and *so also for the quality of life of all of us*, is lining up daily, and getting ever worse.

'Social inequalities would have made the inventors of the modern project blush with shame' conclude Michel Rocard, Dominique Bourg and Floran Augagner in their article 'Human species, endangered' in *Le Monde* of 3 April 2011. In the era of the Enlightenment, in the lifetimes of Francis Bacon, Descartes or even Hegel, the standard of living anywhere on earth was never more than twice as high as in its poorest region. Today, the richest country, Qatar, boasts an income per head 428 times higher than that in the poorest, Zimbabwe. And these are, let's not forget, comparisons between *averages* – and so akin to the facetious recipe for hare-and-horsemeat pâté: take one hare and one horse . . .

The stubborn persistence of poverty on a planet in the throes of economic growth fundamentalism is enough to make thoughtful people pause and reflect on the direct as much as the collateral casualties of that redistribution of wealth. The deepening abyss separating the poor and prospectless from the well-off, sanguine, self-confident and boisterous – an abyss of a depth already exceeding the ability of any but the most muscular and the least scrupulous hiker to scale – is an obvious reason to be gravely concerned. As Rocard and his co-authors warn, the prime victim of deepening inequality will be democracy, as the increasingly scarce, rare and inaccessible paraphernalia of survival and an acceptable life become the object of cut-throat rivalry (and perhaps wars) between the provided-for and the abandoned needy.

One of the basic moral justifications for free market economics, namely that *the pursuit of individual profit also provides the best mechanism for the pursuit of the common good,* has thereby been cast in doubt and all but belied. In the two decades preceding the start of the latest financial crisis, across the great bulk of the nations in the OECD (the Organisation for Economic Co-operation and Development, which presents itself on its website as an association of thirty-four member states that 'span the globe, from North and South America to Europe and the Asia-Pacific region. They include many of the world's most advanced countries but also emerging countries like Mexico, Chile and Turkey. We also work closely with emerging giants like China, India and Brazil and developing economies in Africa, Asia, Latin America and the Caribbean. Together, our goal continues to be to build a stronger, cleaner, fairer world'), the real house-hold incomes for the top 10 per cent grew much faster than for the poorest 10 per cent. In some countries, real incomes of those at the bottom have actually fallen. Income disparities have therefore widened markedly. 'In the US, the average income of the top 10 per cent is now 14 times the bottom 10 per cent' is the admission of Jeremy Warner, assistant editor of the *Daily Telegraph*, one of the newspapers with long records of enthusiastic affirmation of the dexterity and proficiency of the 'invisible hand' of markets, trusted by the editors and subscribers alike to resolve as many problems as markets create (if not more). And he adds: 'Growing income inequality, though obviously undesirable from a social perspective, doesn't necessarily matter if everyone is getting richer together. But when most of the rewards of economic progress are going to a comparatively small number of already high income earners, which is what's been happening in practice, there's plainly going to be a problem.'[2]

That admission, gingerly made and half-hearted as it sounds, and feeling no more than half-true as it in fact is, arrives on the crest of a rising tide of research findings and official statistics documenting the fast-growing distance that separates those at the top from those at the bottom of the social hierarchy. In jarring opposition to political pronouncements intended to be recycled into popular belief – no longer reflected upon, questioned or checked – *the wealth amassed at the top of society has blatantly failed to 'trickle down' and make the rest of us any richer or feel more secure and more optimistic about our and our children's future, or any happier . . .*

In human history, inequality with its all too visible propensity for extended and accelerated self-reproduction is hardly news (as testified by the quotation from St Matthew's Gospel at the beginning of this book). And yet recently the perennial issue of inequality, as well as of its causes and consequences, has been brought back into the focus of public attention, making it into a topic of passionate debates, by quite novel, spectacular, shocking and eye-opening departures.

1   Just how unequal are we today?

Let me start, however, with a few figures illustrating the grandiosity of those departures.

The most seminal among the departures is the discovery, or rather the somewhat delayed realization, that the 'big divide' in American, British and a growing number of other societies 'is now less between the top, the middle and the bottom, than between a tiny group at the very top and nearly everyone else'.[3] For instance, 'the number of billionaires in the US multiplied 40 times in the 25 years to 2007 – whereas the aggregate wealth of the 400 richest Americans rose from $169 to $1500 billion'. After 2007, during the years of credit collapse followed by economic depression and rising unemployment, the tendency acquired a truly exponential pace: rather than hitting everyone in equal measure as had been widely expected and portrayed, the scourge proved to be ruggedly and tenaciously selective in the distribution of its blows: in 2011 the number of billionaires in the US reached its historical record to date of 1,210, while their combined wealth has grown from $3,500 billion in 2007 to $4,500 billion in 2010. 'In 1990, you needed a fortune of £50 million to make it into the list of the 200 richest residents in Britain compiled annually by the *Sunday Times*. By 2008, that figure had soared to £430 million, a near-nine-fold increase.'[4] All in all, 'the combined wealth of the world's richest 1000 people is almost twice as much as the poorest 2.5 billion'. According to the Helsinki-based World Institute for Development Economics Research, people in the richest 1 per cent of the world population are now almost 2,000 times richer than the bottom 50 per cent.[5]

Having recently collated available estimates of global inequality, Danilo Zolo concluded that 'very little data is needed to dramatically confirm that the sun is setting on the "Age of Rights" in the globalization era. The International Labour

Organization estimates that 3 billion people are now living below the poverty line, set at US$2 per day.'[6] As Zolo also pointed out, John Galbraith, in the preface to the *Human Development Report* of the United Nations Development Programme in 1998, documented that 20 per cent of the world's population cornered 86 per cent of all goods and services produced worldwide, while the poorest 20 per cent of them consumed only 1.3 per cent; while today, after nearly fifteen years, these figures have gone from bad to worse: the richest 20 per cent of the population consumes 90 per cent of the goods produced, while the poorest 20 per cent consumes 1 per cent. It is also estimated that the twenty richest people in the world have resources equal to those of the billion poorest people.

Ten years ago Glenn Firebaugh noted that a long-standing trend in worldwide inequality showed signs of reversing – from rising inequality across nations and constant or declining inequality within nations, to declining inequality *across nations* and rising inequality *within them*.[7] While the 'developing' or 'emergent' national economies scored a massive influx of capital in search of new 'virgin lands' promising

8

a quick profit and populated by cheap and meek labour as yet uncontaminated by the bacillus of consumerism and ready to work for bare-survival wages, workplaces in the 'developed' economies vanished at an accelerated pace, leaving local labour forces in fast-deteriorating bargaining positions. Ten years later, François Bourguignon found out that while planetary inequality (between national economies) as measured by average income per head is so far continuing to shrink, the distance between the global richest and the global poorest is continuing to grow, and income differentials inside countries are continuing to expand.[8]

When Érik Orsenna was interviewed by Monique Atlan and Roger-Pol Droit, the economist and novelist winner of the Prix Goncourt summed up the message conveyed by all these and many other similar figures. He insisted that recent transformations have benefited only an infinitely small minority of the world's population; their genuine scale would elude us if we were to confine our analysis, as we used to do only a decade ago, to the average gains of the top 10 per cent.[9] To comprehend the mechanism of the present, ongoing *mutation* (as distinct from a mere 'phase in a cycle'), one needs to focus on the top 1 per cent, perhaps even the top 0.1 per cent. Failing to do so would miss the true impact of the change, which consists in *the degradation of 'middle classes' to the ranks of the 'precariat'*.

That suggestion is confirmed by every study, whether it focuses on the researcher's own country or comes from far and wide. In addition, however, all studies agree on yet another point: *almost everywhere in the world inequality is growing fast and that means that the rich, and particularly the very rich, get richer, whereas the poor, and particularly the very poor, get poorer* – most certainly in relative, but in a growing number of cases also in absolute, terms. Moreover, people who are rich are getting richer just *because* they are rich. People who are poor get poorer just *because* they are poor. Nowadays, inequality goes on deepening *by its own logic and momentum*. It needs no other help or kick from outside – no outside stimuli, pressures, or blows. Social inequality nowadays seems ever closer to turning into the first perpetuum mobile in history – which humans, after innumerable failed attempts, have finally managed to invent and set in motion. This is the second among the departures that obliges us to think about social inequality from a new perspective.

As long ago as 1979 a Carnegie study vividly demonstrated what an enormous amount of evidence available at that time suggested and common life experience continued daily to confirm: that each child's future was largely determined by the child's social circumstances, by the geographical place of its birth and its parents' place in the society of its birth – and not by its own brains, talents, efforts and dedication. The son of a big company lawyer was twenty-seven times more likely than the son of a minor official employed on and off (both sons sitting on the same bench in the same class, doing equally well, studying with the same dedication and boasting the same IQ) to be paid a salary by the age of forty that would put him in the top 10 per cent of the richest people in the country; his classmate would have only a one in eight chance of earning even a median income. Less than three decades later, in 2007, things had got much worse – the gap had widened and deepened, becoming less bridgeable than ever before. A study by the Congressional Budget Office found that the wealth of the richest 1 per cent of Americans totalled $16.8 trillion, 2 trillion more than the combined wealth of the bottom 90 per cent of the population. According to the Center for American Progress, during those three decades the average income of the bottom 50 per cent of Americans grew by 6 per cent – while the income of the top 1 per cent increased by 229 per cent.[10]

In 1960, the average pay after taxes for a chief executive at the largest US corporations was 12 times greater than the average wage of factory workers. By 1974, the CEO's salary and perks had gone up to about 35 times the pay of the company's average worker. In 1980 the average CEO was already making 42 times as much as the average blue-collar worker, doubling ten years later to 84 times. But then, in about 1980, a hyper-acceleration of inequality took off. By the mid-1990s, according to *Business Week*, the factor was already 135 times; in 1999 it had reached 400-fold and in 2000 jumped again to 531 . . .[11] And these are only a few of a fast-growing number of similar 'facts of the matter' and of figures attempting to grasp, quantify and measure them. One can go on quoting them endlessly, as there is no shortage of new figures which each successive research study adds to the mass already accumulated.

What are the social realities, however, which those figures reflect?

This is how Joseph Stiglitz sums up the revelations from the dramatic aftermath of arguably the two or three most prosperous decades in a row in the history of capitalism that preceded the 2007 credit collapse, and of the depression that followed: inequality has always been justified on the grounds that those at the top contributed more to the economy, performing the role of 'job creators', but 'then came 2008 and 2009, and you saw these guys who brought the economy to the brink of ruin walking off with hundreds of millions of dollars'. Most obviously, you couldn't this time justify the rewards in terms of their beneficiaries' contribution to society; what the latter contributed was not new jobs, but lengthening lines of '*redundant* people' (as the jobless are now dubbed, not without sound reasons). In his book *The Price of Inequality*, Stiglitz warns that the US is becoming a country 'in which the rich live in gated communities, send their children to expensive schools and have access to first-rate medical care. Meanwhile, the rest live in a world marked by insecurity, at best mediocre education and in effect rationed health care.[12] This is a *picture of two worlds*, with few if any interfaces or meeting points between them, and so also with their inter-communication all but broken (in the US as much as in Britain, families have started to set aside an ever greater part of their income to cover the costs of living geographically as well as socially away – the further away the better – from 'other people', and particularly the poor among them).

In his sharp and brilliant vivisection of the present state of inequality, Daniel Dorling, Professor of Human Geography at Sheffield University, puts flesh on the bones of Stiglitz's skeleton synthesis, while simultaneously raising the perspective from a single country to the planetary level:

The poorest tenth of the world's population regularly go hungry. The richest tenth cannot remember a time of hunger in their family's history. The poorest tenth can only rarely secure the most basic education for their children; the richest tenth are concerned to pay sufficient school fees to ensure that their children need only mix with their so-called 'equals' and 'betters' and because they have come to fear their children mixing with other children. The poorest tenth almost always live in places where there is no social security, no unemployment benefit. The richest tenth cannot imagine themselves ever having to try to live on those benefits. The poorest tenth can only secure day work in town, or are peasants in rural areas; the richest tenth cannot imagine not having a secure monthly salary. Above them, the top fraction of a per cent, the very richest cannot imagine surviving on a salary rather than on the income coming from the interest that their wealth generates.[13]

And he concludes: 'as people polarize geographically, they begin to know less and less of each other and imagine more and more'.[14]

At the same time, in his most recent statement, called 'Inequality: the real cause of our economic woes', Stewart Lansey falls in with the verdicts of Stiglitz and Dorling that the power-assisted dogma that credits the rich with rendering service to society by getting richer is nothing more than a blend of a purposeful lie with a contrived moral blindness:

According to economic orthodoxy, a stiff dose of inequality brings more efficient and faster growing economies. This is because higher rewards and lower taxes at the top – it is claimed – boost entrepreneurialism and deliver a larger economic pie.

So has the 30-year experiment in boosting inequality worked? The evidence suggests no. The wealth gap has soared, but without the promised economic progress. Since 1980, UK growth and productivity rates have been a third lower and unemployment five times higher than in the more egalitarian post-war era. The three post-1980 recessions have been deeper and longer than those of the 1950s and 1960s, culminating in the crisis of the last four years. The main outcome of the post-1980 experiment has been an economy that is more polarized and more prone to crisis.[15]

Having noted that 'falling wage shares suck demand out of economies which are heavily dependent on consumer spending' so that, in effect, 'consumer societies lose the capacity to consume', and that 'concentrating the proceeds of growth in the hands of a small global financial elite leads to asset bubbles', Lansey comes to an inevitable conclusion: *the harsh realities of social inequality are bad for everyone or almost everyone within society.* And he suggests a sentence that ought to have followed such a verdict, yet thus far has not: 'The central lesson of the last 30 years is that an economic model that allows the richest members of society to accumulate a larger and larger share of the cake will eventually self-destruct. It is a lesson, it appears, that has yet to be learned.'

It is a lesson we need to learn and learn it we must lest we reach the point of no return: the moment when the current 'economic model', having given out so many warnings of approaching catastrophe yet having failed to capture our attention and to prompt us to act, fulfils its 'self-destructive' potential. Richard Wilkinson and Kate Pickett, the authors of an eye-opening study, *The Spirit Level: Why More Equal Societies Almost Always Do Better*,[16] point out in their jointly written foreword to Dorling's book that the belief that 'paying the rich huge salaries and bonuses' is right because their 'rare talents' benefit the rest of society is a straightforward lie. A lie which we swallow with equanimity only at our peril – and, eventually, at the cost of our self-destruction . . .

Since the appearance of the study by Wilkinson and Pickett the evidence of the detrimental and quite often devastating impact of high and rising levels of inequality on pathologies of human cohabitation, and the gravity of social problems, has only accrued and goes on accruing. The correlation between high levels of income inequality and a growing volume of social pathologies has now been amply confirmed. An increasing number of researchers and analysts point out, too, that in addition to its negative impact on the quality of life, inequality has also an adverse effect on economic performance; instead of enhancing it, it holds it back. In the study already quoted, Bourguignon picks some of the causes of the latter phenomenon: potential entrepreneurs being deprived of access to bank credit because they lack the collateral that creditors require, or the rising costs of education that strip talented youngsters of the chance to acquire the skills they need to develop and apply their abilities. He adds the negative impact of the rise in social tensions and the ambience of insecurity – the fast-growing costs of security services eating into resources that could be turned to better economic uses.[17]

And so, to sum up: is there truth in what so many of us believe, and what all of us are pressed and nudged to believe and all too often feel tempted, and inclined, to accept? Is it, to sum up, true that 'the richness of the few benefits us all'? Is it true, in particular, that any tampering with the natural inequality of humans is harmful to the health and vigour of society, as well as to its creative and productive powers which each and every human member of society has a vested interest in magnifying and holding at the highest conceivable level? And is it true that the differentiation of social positions, capacities, entitlements and rewards reflects the differences in the natural endowments and the contributions of its members to the well-being of society?

The rest of the argument will attempt to show why those and similar beliefs are lies and why they stand little if any chance of ever turning into truths and delivering on their (deceitful) promise. It will also attempt to find out why, despite the ever more evident untruth of those beliefs, we go on overlooking the duplicity of their promise and fail to see through the utter unlikelihood that they will deliver.

2 Why do we put up with inequality?

In his study of inequality, its manifestations and causes, Daniel Dorling emphatically points out that 'social inequality within rich countries persists because of a continued belief in the tenets of injustice, and it can be shock for people to realize that there might be something wrong with much of the ideological fabric of the society we live in'.[18] Those 'tenets of injustice' are tacit (implicit) premises underpinning and pretending to 'make sense' of the loudly voiced (explicit) convictions, but they are hardly ever reflected upon and subjected to tests; they are the always intimated, but seldom articulated beliefs *with* which we think – but *of* which we do not think when forming opinions that have no other, bony and fleshy, legs to stand on.

Take for instance, as Dorling does, the pronouncement made in 1970 on her visit to the United States by Margaret Thatcher, who was known to make political capital out of the popular prejudices she was uniquely keen and flawlessly apt to spot:

> One of the reasons that we value individuals is not because they're all the same, but because they're all different . . . I would say, let our children grow tall and some taller than others if they have the ability in them to do so. Because we must build a society in which each citizen can develop his full potential, both for his own benefit and for the community as a whole.

Note that the crucial premise making Thatcher's statement appear well-nigh self-evident – the supposition that 'community as a whole' is properly served by each citizen serving 'his own benefit' – was not spelled out explicitly and was here taken for granted. And as Dorling observes acidly, Thatcher assumes that 'ability potential was to be treated like height' (that is, something beyond the power of humans to tamper with) – as well as presuming, again without proof, that different individuals have different abilities *by nature* rather than having different capacities to develop their potential because they are cast in different *social conditions*. In other words, Thatcher takes it for granted, as something self-evident, that our different abilities, just like our different heights, are determined at birth, thereby 'normalizing' the implication that there is little or nothing in human power to change such a verdict of fate. This was one of the reasons why, by the end of the last century, 'the strange notion that by acting selfishly people benefit others in some way became accepted'.[19]

This is not, however, the only 'tenet of injustice' that in Dorling's opinion underpins and sustains the persistence of inequality. He names several other tacit and latent convictions that – despite failing every proof of reality, or without having been given the chance of critical testing – obstinately go on shaping our popular perceptions, attitudes and actions. Among such 'tenets of injustice' Dorling lists the belief that (1) elitism is efficient (because the good of the many can be enhanced only by promoting abilities which relatively few, by definition, solely possess); that (2) exclusion is both normal and necessary for society's health, while greed is good for life's improvement; and that (3) the resulting despair is inevitable and cannot be avoided. It is this collection of false beliefs that means that our collective misery caused by our voluntary and almost unreflective and perfunctory submission to social inequality carries on and indeed self-perpetuates:

> People have been making their own history for quite some time, despite repeatedly lamenting and finding themselves in circumstances not of their choosing. And the histories are made collectively – we collectively gorge now on shopping and soap operas. Status paranoia is reinforced as our people watching is done through watching television and surfing the Internet. Being greedy is offered to us collectively through advertising as a lure to wanting more.[20]

To cut a long story short, most of us most of the time willingly (sometimes joyously, at some other times grudgingly, railing and gnashing our teeth) embrace the offer and abandon ourselves to the lifelong task of making the best of it. Is it enough, however, to change one's mind to change one's ways, and is changing one's ways enough to change the reality and its stark demands under which we act?

It is true that, like it or not, we belong to the species of *homo eligens*: the *choosing* animal; and that no amount of pressure, however coercive, cruel and indomitable, has ever managed or is ever likely to manage to completely suppress our choices and thus unambiguously and indomitably determine our conduct. We are not billiard balls moved on the table wherever the cue holder sends us; we are, so to speak, *doomed to be free* – and however keenly we may desire to be liberated from the torments of choice, we will forever face more than one way to proceed. There are two largely autonomous factors that between themselves shape our selections, our way of living and our life's trajectory. One is 'fate', a class of circumstances over which we have no influence: things 'happening to us' that are not of our doing (such as the geographical place and the social location into which we are born, or the time of our birth). The other factor is our character, which we are, at least in principle, able to influence – to work on, train and cultivate. 'Fate' determines the range of our realistic options, but it is ultimately our character which chooses between them.

Of course, the range of 'realistic' options set by 'fate' differ, often sharply, by the degree of their realism. Some options are, or at least look, easier to pick up and follow than some others being or appearing to be safer, less risky bets and/or more attractive choices; their chances of being chosen are therefore likely to be greater than those of their alternative, currently unpopular (and so perceived as unadvisable) choices, which may be suspected of requiring greater time and more cumbersome effort, of calling for more sacrifice, or of carrying the risk of public condemnation and loss of prestige – as they most often do. The distribution of the probabilities of the 'realistic' options to be picked up therefore also belongs to the realm of 'fate': we live after all in a 'structured' social environment, and the 'structuring' consists precisely of the manipulation of probabilities. It consists of arranging and rearranging the assignment of rewards and punishments in such a fashion as to make the probability of some choices much higher, and of some others much lower, than they otherwise would have been. 'Reality', after all, is the name we give to the external resistance to our own inner wishes . . . The stronger their resistance, the more 'real' the obstacles feel.

The higher the social cost of a choice, the less is its probability of being chosen. And the costs of a refusal to do what the choosers are pressed to do, as well as the rewards for obedience in choosing, are paid primarily in the precious currency of social acceptance, position and prestige. In our society these costs are arranged in a way that renders resistance to inequality and its consequences (public and personal alike) highly difficult and therefore less likely to be undertaken and pursued than its alternatives: a placid and resigned submission or willing collaboration. And the dice which we, denizens of the capitalist, individualized society of consumers, must go on casting over and over again in all or most of our life games are in most cases loaded in favour of those who benefit or hope to benefit from inequality . . .

3   Some big lies on which a bigger one floats

John Maxwell Coetzee, a formidable philosopher and exquisite novelist as well as an indefatigable and acute recorder of our world's sins, blunders and inanities, notes that

> the assertion, that our world must be divided into competing economic entities because this is what its nature demands, is far-fetched. Competitive economies have come to be because we decided to give them this shape. Competition is a sublimated substitute for war. War is in no way inevitable. If we want war, we may choose war, but if we want peace, we may equally well choose peace. If we wish rivalry, we may choose rivalry; we can, however, decide instead on friendly cooperation.[21]

The snag, though, is that whether or not it has been shaped by the decisions taken and implemented by our ancestors, our world at the beginning of the twenty-first century is not hospitable to peaceful coexistence, let alone human solidarity and friendly cooperation. It has been so shaped that it renders cooperation and solidarity not just an unpopular, but also a difficult and costly choice. No wonder that relatively few people, and on relatively few occasions, find it in their material and/or spiritual power to take and see through such a choice. The great majority of people, however noble and lofty their beliefs and intentions, find themselves confronted with hostile and vengeful, and above all indomitable realities; realities of omnipresent cupidity and corruption, rivalry and selfishness on all sides, and for all those reasons realities counselling and extolling mutual suspicion and perpetual vigilance. People can't change such realities single-handedly, wish them away, argue them away or ignore them – and so they are left with little alternative but to follow the patterns of behaviour which, knowingly or not, by design or by default, monotonously reproduce the world of *bellum omnium contra omnes*. This is why we all too often mistake those realities (contrived, implanted or imagined realities forced with our help to reproduce daily) for the 'nature of things', which no human power can challenge and reform. To follow Coetzee's argument once more: 'an average human' will go on believing that the world is ruled by necessity and not by an abstract moral code. He or she will continue to believe what that 'average human' has, let us frankly admit, more than enough sound reasons to believe: that what must be, must be – full stop. This is the world in which one needs to live one's life, we tend to (rightly) conclude. To that kind of world, we (wrongly) deduce, there is no – there can't be – an alternative.

So what are those ostensible 'musts', which we, the 'average people' (or, simply, 'the ordinary folk') deem to be 'in the order' or 'in the nature' of things and bound to stay like that? In other words, what are they, the tacitly accepted premises invisibly present in every opinion about 'the state of the world' to which we commonly attach ourselves and which shape our understanding (more correctly, *misunderstanding*) of that world – but which we seldom if ever try earnestly to scrutinize, see through and test against the evidence?

Let me name just a few of them, though perhaps those that more than all the other false beliefs bear responsibility for the bane of social inequality and its apparently unstoppable growth and cancer-like metastases. But let me warn you from the start that under somewhat closer scrutiny, all those alleged 'musts' will reveal themselves to be nothing other than various aspects of the status quo – of things as they *do*, but in no way *must*, stand at the moment; and that those aspects of our current plight are also, in their turn, sustained by untested, unsound or downright misleading premises. It is true that they are now 'realities', in the sense that they staunchly resist attempts to reform or replace them; more precisely, any attempts that are, and can conceivably be, undertaken with the tools presently at our disposal (as two great sociologists, W. I. Thomas and Florian Znaniecki, found out a century ago: if people believe something to be true, they make it true by the way they behave . . .). This in no way proves that the reform or replacement of the aspects in question is unachievable, however – staying *permanently* beyond human power. At the utmost, it may suggest that changing them would require *more than a mere change of mind*. It would call for nothing less than a change, quite often a drastic and initially painful and off-putting change, in *the way we live*.

A few such tacit presumptions commonly accepted as 'obvious' (needing no proof) that have been selected here for closer scrutiny are the following:

1 *Economic growth* is the only way to handle the challenges and possibly to resolve all and any problems that human cohabitation is bound to generate.

2 *Perpetually rising consumption*, or more precisely an accelerating rotation of novel objects of consumption, is perhaps the sole, or at any rate the principal and most effective, way to gratify the human pursuit of happiness.

3 *Inequality of humans is natural*, and adjusting human life chances to its inevitability benefits us all, while tampering with its precepts is bound to bring harm to all.

4 *Rivalry* (with its two sides: the elevation of the worthy and the exclusion/degradation of the

unworthy) is simultaneously a necessary and the sufficient condition of social justice as well as of the reproduction of social order.

Economic growth

'It's the economy, stupid' is a phrase coined by James Carville, a strategist of Bill Clinton's 1992 presidential campaign against George H. W. Bush. In the years since its coinage, this phrase has had a spectacular career in the worldwide political vocabulary. It is firmly settled by now in the language of politics as well in the 'doxa' (that is, the assembly of beliefs used routinely by the lay public to think with, but seldom if ever thought about, let alone scrutinized and tested), cropping up again and again in the speeches of politicians and the briefings of spin doctors during successive electoral campaigns – or if need be without these or any other occasions. The phrase assumes, as a self-evident fact of life proved by common experience beyond reasonable doubt, that public sentiments, sympathies or antipathies, public willingness to offer or to deny support to the adversaries engaged in electoral battles, and the inclination of voters to recognize their interests in electoral programmes and slogans are all fully or almost fully determined by the meanders of 'economic growth'. It assumes that whatever other values and preferences voters might hold, it is the presence or absence of 'economic growth' that tends to guide their choices more than any other consideration. What follows is that the figures supposed to measure the degree of economic growth are the most reliable predictors of the electoral chances of the rivals for occupation of the corridors of power. The same expectation is often expressed through another popular phrase, 'vote with your pocketbook' (in American English) or 'with your wallet' (in British English) – a natural human disposition which, according to Longman Dictionary, means 'to vote for someone or something you think will help you have the most money'.

This may be the case, given our recently widespread and by now firmly entrenched conviction that it is on the things which the official figures of 'economic growth' ostensibly measure that the chances of a decent, gratifying and dignified life – in short, of a life worth living – primarily depend. The snag, however, is that this conviction is neither innate nor in any other way 'natural' to humans; on the contrary, it is of relatively recent origin. The most formidable minds among the pioneers of modern economics considered 'economic growth' a regrettable nuisance rather than a blessing: though, fortunately, a temporary and eminently transient irritant, caused by an *as yet insufficient* supply of the goods indispensable for satisfying the sum total of human needs. Most of them believed that such a sum total could be calculated – and once the productive capacity of society matched it, the 'stable' or 'steady' economy, more akin and friendly to the 'natural' disposition of human beings, would follow. John Stuart Mill, a pioneer of modern economic thought and one of the most gifted philosophers and scholars of the nineteenth century,[22] anticipated for instance the inevitable, indeed matter-of-fact, transition from economic *growth* to a '*stationary* state'. In his magnum opus, *Principles of Political Economy*, he wrote, as anyone can read in the current edition of Wikipedia, that 'increase of wealth is not boundless. The end of growth leads to a stationary state. The stationary state of capital and wealth . . . would be a very considerable improvement on our present condition.' And:

A stationary condition of capital and population implies no stationary state of human improvement. There would be as much scope as ever for all kinds of mental culture, and moral and social progress; as much room for improving the art of living, and much more likelihood of it being improved, when minds ceased to be engrossed by the art of getting on.'[23]

While well into the last century, as also can be read in Wikipedia, John Maynard Keynes, one of the most influential economists of the twentieth century,[24] still expected the day to inevitably arrive when society could focus on *ends* (happiness and well-being, for example) rather than, as hitherto, on *means* (economic growth and the individual pursuit of profit). He wrote that 'avarice is a vice, the exaction of usury is a misdemeanor, and the love of money is detestable . . . We shall once more value ends above means and prefer the good to the useful.'[25] And insisted that 'the day is not far off when the economic problem will take the back seat where it belongs, and the arena of the heart and the head will be occupied or reoccupied, by our real problems –

the problems of life and of human relations, of creation and behaviour and religion'[26] – in other words, problems that are not only 'real', but immensely nobler and more attractive than the needs of 'mere survival' guiding economic preoccupations to date or the temptations of aggrandisement waiting to supplant them; problems that, when finally earnestly confronted, open the road to a *genuinely wholesome mode of human life and human cohabitation.*

Sixty more years have passed of the unbridled capitalist pursuit of wealth for its own sake, a chase during which the view of public wealth as a tool for the construction of a society hospitable to the diverse, multifaceted demands of a good human life, worthy of being lived, was dismissed and neglected. Now Robert and Edward Skidelsky have published a study called *How Much Is Enough? Money and the Good Life.*[27] In Michael O'Leary's rendition in his essay under the tell-all title of 'Drowned by the rising tides',[28] it concludes that 'the myth that the rising tide lifts all boats does not fool anyone today' (a somewhat premature observation, alas, as the fooling in question seems to be still in full swing, contrary to the authors' expectation of a sobering-up effect of the most recent and most shattering evidence that global inequality is rising at an unprecedented speed). The 2012 edition of the OECD's annual report, 'Going for growth', suggests, in O'Leary's view, that 'it's the poor that gets the blame but the rich what gets the pleasure' in official interpretations of the roots of the present troubles. While John Evans, the General Secretary of the Trade Union Advisory Committee, comments that

> Going for Growth fails to draw lessons from the crisis and continues to press for deregulated labour markets. Policies that contribute to the current crisis are presented as solutions. It's particularly worrying that the OECD recommends reducing protection for workers, at a time when greater confidence is needed.

The 'invisible hand of the market', fancifully reputed to act in favour of universal welfare – the hand which the state policy of deregulation is meant to liberate from the legal handcuffs previously designed to limit its freedom of movement – may indeed be invisible, but there is little doubt to whom that hand belongs and who directs its moves. 'Deregulation' of banks and of the movement of capital allows the rich to move freely, to seek and find the best, most profit-generating terrains for exploitation and so to get richer – whereas the 'deregulation' of labour markets renders the poor unable to follow the exploits, let alone to arrest or at least slow down the peregrinations of the owners of capital (renamed 'investors' in stock-exchange parlance), and so is bound to make them poorer. In addition to the damage done to their level of income, their chances of employment and of a living wage are now exposed to the vagaries of wealth-seeking capital, with the prospect of competition making them chronically precarious and turning them into causes of acute spiritual discomfort, perpetual worry and chronic unhappiness – banes that won't go away and won't stop tormenting them even in the (brief) periods of relative safety.

The endemically divisive effects of the 'policy of deregulation' belong among the most closely guarded official secrets, however; in scripts officially composed for public consumption, deregulation is presented as the royal road to the well-being of all; while GNP statistics, ostensibly measuring the ups and downs of the 'total wealth' of the nation and identified with the nation's well-being, keep silent about the way in which that wealth is distributed. They hide it instead of laying it bare; in particular and most importantly, the truth which those statistics prevent from being outed is that an *increase in 'total wealth' goes hand in hand with a deepening of social inequality* while stretching yet more the already unbridgeable gap between the existential security and general well being of the top end and the bottom end of the social pyramid. And let's recall that the topmost part of that pyramid is getting narrower year in year out, while the rest of it, all the way down to the bottom, unstoppably expands . . .

Indeed, nearly all the increase in the gross national product that has been achieved in the US since the credit collapse in 2007, more than 90 per cent of it, has been appropriated by the richest 1 per cent of Americans. The widening of the gap, and the shrinking of the band of multibillionaires who appropriate the lion's share of 'economic growth', go on seemingly unstoppably and at a steadily accelerating pace, as Julia Kollewe recently computed. Just ten of the world's richest have by now accumulated wealth of $2.7 trillion, about the same size as the French economy, the fifth biggest in the world.[29] One of them, Amancio Ortega, founder of Inditex, owner of 1,600 Zara stores, has added $18 billion to his wealth in just the twelve months since October 2011, which comes out at about $66 million a day. According to data authoritatively endorsed by the High Pay Commission in Britain, the earnings of top executives in that country grew by 40 times in the last thirty years, while average wages in the country only tripled and have now stopped at the £25,900 level. In the opinion of Deborah Hargreaves, the Commission's chairperson, 'there is a crisis at the top of British business and it is deeply corrosive to our economy. When pay for senior executives is set behind closed doors, does not reflect company success and is fuelling massive inequality, it represents a deep malaise at the very top of our society.' The fabulous growth in the fortunes of a section of society 0.1 per cent strong occurs, to rub salt into the wound, 'in a time of unparalleled austerity' for most of the remaining 99.9 per cent.

The comparisons above reflect the growing inequality in the populations confined inside single nation-states; but as for the global dimension of inequality, Professor Anja Weiss of Duisburg-Essen University, in collating and extrapolating current trends, derives a very similar, if not even more sombre and off-putting, indeed gruesome, prospect: 'A realist picture of future global inequality is stark. If things remain as they are there is little incentive or chance for change . . . In a realist perspective it is likely that inequalities continue and that the nation state system continues to legitimize them.'[30]

The overall picture leaves little if any room for doubt: as things stand today, economic growth (as depicted in the statistics of 'gross national product' and identified with the rising amount of money changing hands) does not for most of us augur a better future to come. Instead, it portends for an already overwhelming and fast-rising number of people yet deeper and starker inequality, a yet more precarious condition and so also more degradation, chagrin, affront and humiliation – an ever tougher struggle for social survival. The enrichment of the rich does not 'trickle down' even to those located in their closest vicinity in the hierarchies of wealth and income – let alone to those further down the ladder; the notorious though increasingly illusionary 'ladder' of upward mobility is turning more and more into a stack of impermeable grids and impassable barriers. *Economic growth' signals rising opulence for a few, but a steep fall in social standing and self-esteem for an uncountable mass of others.* Instead of passing the test of a universal solution to the most ubiquitous, obtrusive and harrowing social problems, 'economic growth' as we've come to know it from our collective, increasingly unwholesome experience looks suspiciously like the principal cause of the persistence and aggravation of those problems.

And yet . . . The fabulous incomes, bonuses and perks drawn by the 'executive officers' of big corporations continue all too often to be justified in terms of the notorious 'trickle-down theory': the claim that successful entrepreneurs in the manner of Steve Jobs or Richard Branson will create successful companies and thereby create more jobs, and that, with such uniquely talented people being few and far between, the boards of big companies need to offer top salaries to top people in order to do good service to the nation (well, to their stockholders in the first and the last place . . .); otherwise the 'wealth creators' would take their talents elsewhere, to the detriment of everybody who might have benefited from the company's good (read: profitable in royalties terms) performance. Persons like Steve Jobs or Richard Branson are indeed few and far between – which cannot be said, however, about the fabulous salaries which people admitted to the magic circle of big companies' big fishes have come to expect matter-of-factly, whether they lead the companies they are appointed to rule to a string of victories or to a catastrophe. The celebrated names cropping up whenever the 'trickle-down' arguments are heard serve as fig leaves to cover up the tacit, unwritten collective insurance policy which the elite of the super-rich have managed to secure for themselves whatever their performance . . .

For all practical intents and purposes, that policy cuts their entitlement to riches free from any benefits they may or may not bring to those whose welfare they are meant to promote – instead of inducing and enhancing, let alone guaranteeing, a rise in the production of public wealth. The genuine purpose of the policy is to *secure privileges*, not to harness them to public service. Its effect is the exemption of a narrow group of top earners from the impact of whatever calamity their activities might have visited on all those whose livelihood they've exposed to the vagaries of fate. The stake here is not the *production* of wealth, but its *distribution*; more to the point, the rendering of the CEOs' monopoly on high earnings independent from and unrelated to the quality of the performance which those earnings were supposed to reward. In the event that the CEO's stock-exchange gambles are miscalculated, those whose jobs they were meant to make secure are made redundant, lose their livelihood and are denied living wages – but the CEO can look joyously towards a contractually guaranteed 'golden handshake'. According to Wikipedia's summary of that practice,

> 'golden handshakes' are offered only to high-ranking executives by major corporations and may entail a value measured in millions of dollars. Golden handshakes are given to offset the risk inherent in taking the new job, since high-ranking executives have a high likelihood

of being fired and since a company requiring an outsider to come in at such a high level may be in a precarious financial position. Their use has caused some investors concern since they do not specify that the executive had to perform well. In some high-profile instances, executives cashed in their stock options, while under their stewardship their companies lost millions of dollars and thousands of workers were laid off. Golden handshakes may create perverse incentives for top executives to facilitate the sale of the company they are managing by artificially reducing its stock price.

Below are just a few recent, randomly selected examples of the by now universal practice:

Upon their departure from a company, well-heeled executives tend to have severance packages worth millions. In many cases, such package deals are payable regardless of whether the company meets its financial objectives or is even profitable. . . . For example the severance package awarded to Michael Ovitz, former president of The Walt Disney Co., totalled more than $140 million, which was about 10% of Disney's total annual net income. Or consider the $40 million that chief executive Jill Barad received from Mattel Inc. She was fired because the company's stock had dropped more than 50%.[31]

Sir Ian Blair is in line for an astonishing £1 million pay-off after being ousted as head of Scotland Yard, it emerged yesterday. The Metropolitan Police Commissioner's reward for his bungled reign is a golden handshake of about £295,000 – the remainder of his salary had he fulfilled his five-year contract. A further £100,000 covers perks he would have been entitled to had he remained Met chief until February 2010, when he was originally scheduled to step down, and his legal costs. On top of this Sir Ian will receive a lump sum pension payout of £672,000 and an index-linked pension of £126,000 a year. The deal was described by one MP as 'absurd' and by another as ' ridiculous'. Sir Ian's three and a half years in his post were dogged by questions about his judgment, leadership credentials and politically correct style of policing. He was forced from office last month just hours after he faced damaging new sleaze allegations about police contracts awarded to a close friend.[32]

Let me add that contrary to the assurances voiced by numerous influential economists, including the 1995 Nobel Prize winner Robert Lucas (who in 2003, just a couple of years before the spectacular collapse of the economy guided by banks and credit, announced the deregulation of financial money markets as 'the solution, for all practical purposes' of 'the central problem of depression prevention'), the exorbitant earnings of the already rich, instead of being reinvested in the 'real economy' (that is, the part of economy moved by the production and distribution of life-serving goods), were used to reassign nominal quantities of money inside the magic circle of the very rich uninterested in and unconcerned with services to the 'real economy'. In the words of Stewart Lansey,

> Modern economic theory predicts that pure markets work in a way that benefits the wider economy. Yet it was perverse incentives that led to banks pumping uncontrolled supplies of credit into the global economy. This

enriched a generation of financiers but only by the expansion of activity which stifled the 'real economy' . . . Money poured into take-overs, private equity, property and a variety of forms of speculative activity and financial and industrial engineering that led to an accumu-lation of fortunes but mostly via the transfer of existing rather than the creation of new wealth, businesses and jobs.[33]

From all that, only one conclusion can follow: 'Deregulation and demutualization (of the finan-cial and credit-providing institutions) proved another gravy train for those at the top of the finance industry, bringing higher fees, commis-sions and bonuses'[34] – while desiccating yet further the already meagre assets of the millions of 'credit-beneficiaries' living and working in the 'real economy', as well as dependent on its booms and busts for the prospects of their livelihood.

Rising consumption

'The ultimate goal of technology, the telos of techne', suggested Jonathan Franzen in a com-mencement speech delivered on 21 May 2011 at Kenyon College, 'is to replace a natural world that's indifferent to our wishes – a world of hurricanes and hardships and breakable hearts, a world of resistance – with a world so responsive to our wishes as to be, effectively, a mere extension of the self.' It is all about comfort and convenience, stupid – so the speech suggested: about an effortless comfort and comfortable effortlessness. About making the world obedient and pliable to our whims and fancies; about excising from the world all that might stand, obstinately and pugnaciously, between will and reality. Correction: as what we call 'reality' is what resists human will, it is all about putting paid to reality. Living in a world made only of one's wants and wishes; of mine and yours, of our – the buyers, consumers, users and beneficiaries of technology – wants and wishes.

One wish we all share and feel especially strongly, passionately about is the desire to love and be loved.

Franzen's speech continued:

> As our markets discover and respond to what consumers most want, our technology has become extremely adept at creating products that correspond to our fantasy ideal of an

erotic relationship, in which the beloved object asks for nothing and gives everything, instantly, and makes us feel all-powerful, and doesn't throw terrible scenes when it's replaced by an even sexier object and is consigned to a drawer

– as well as to a dustbin and the bottomless landfill of oblivion, let me add. Increasingly, marketed products of technology, such as electronic gadgets impelled into action at a mere voice command or allowing images to grow bigger by a mere spreading of two fingers, incarnate everything that we'd always dreamt the loved objects would offer but that we seldom if ever managed really to get – with the added invaluable quality of never outstaying their welcome and never kicking back once they have been kicked out. Electronic gadgets do not just serve love: they are designed to be loved in the way that is offered to all other love objects but that they seldom allow. Electronic gadgets are love's most wholesome objects, setting standards and patterns for both entering into and exiting from love affairs that can be ignored by all other love objects, electronic or fleshy, inanimate or animate, only at the peril of being disqualified and rejected.

Unlike in the case of electronic gadgets, however, the love of a human *for a human* means commitment, the acceptance of risks, a readiness for self-sacrifice; it means choosing an uncertain and unmapped, rough and bumpy track, hoping – and being determined – to share life with another. Love may or may not go in a pair with unclouded happiness, but it can hardly ever go in a pair with comfort and convenience; never self-confidently expect it, let alone be certain of it . . . On the contrary, it demands a stretching of one's skills and will to the utmost, and even then portends the possibility of defeat, of an unmasking of one's inadequacy and injury to one's self-esteem. The sanitized, smoothed-out, thorn-free and risk-free product of electronics is anything but love: what it offers is an insurance against 'the dirt', which, as Franzen rightly observed, 'love inevitably splatters on the terror of our self-regard'. The electronically concocted version of love is, in the last account, not at all about love; products of consumer technology catch their clients with the bait of satisfying their narcissism. They promise to reflect well on us – whatever happens and whatever we do or desist from doing. As Franzen pointed out, 'we star in our own movies, we photograph ourselves incessantly, we click the mouse and a machine confirms our sense of mastery . . . To friend a person is merely to include the person in our private hall of flattering mirrors.' But, he added, 'trying to be perfectly likeable is incompatible with a loving relationship'.

Love is, or threatens to be, an antidote against narcissism. It is also the prime whistleblower when it comes to debunking the falsehood of the pretences on which we try to perch our self-esteem while laboriously avoiding testing it in the field of action. What the electronically sterilized and whitewashed, counterfeit version of love truly offers is bet-hedging to protect self-esteem against the hazards for which the genuine article is notorious.

The 'electronic boom', the fabulous profits garnered from the sale of increasingly 'user friendly' gadgets – pliable, submissive, always obedient and never contravening the master's will – bears all the marks of another 'virgin land' freshly discovered and put into exploitation (and a recipe for a never-ending string of new virgin-land discoveries). Consumer markets score another conquest: another area of human concerns, worries, desires and struggles – hitherto left to grass-roots initiatives, cottage industries and home baking and therefore unprofitable marketwise – has now been successfully commoditized and commercialized; activities in that area, as in so many other areas of human preoccupations and activities, have been converted into buying escapades and redirected to the shopping malls. But let me repeat: contrary to its duplicitous claims, the area most recently opened to exploitation by the consumer markets is not one of love – but of narcissism.

All the same, the same messages are coming in from screens and loudspeakers in immense and unabating profusion, day in, day out. Sometimes the messages are boldly explicit, at other times cleverly hidden – but each time, whether aimed at the intellectual faculties, emotions or subconscious desires, they promise, suggest and intimate happiness (or pleasurable sensations, moments of glee, rapture or ecstasy: a hoard of lifelong happiness apportioned and delivered little by little, in daily or hourly doses and in small coins) embedded in the acquisition, possession and enjoyment of the shop-supplied goods.

The message could hardly be clearer: *the road to happiness travels through shopping*; the sum total of the nation's shopping activity is the prime and least fallible measure of society's happiness, and the size of one's individual share in that sum is the prime and least fallible measure of personal happiness. In shops, reliable medicines can be found for everything annoying and inconvenient – for all those big and small nuisances and discomforts of life that stand in the way of a cosy, comfortable and uninterruptedly gratifying mode of being. Whatever they otherwise advertise, display and sell, shops are pharmacies for every genuine and putative trouble of life, those already suffered and those feared to lie ahead.

The message is sent indiscriminately: to those at the top and at the bottom of the pile alike. The message is presumed to be universal – valid for every life occasion and every human being. In practice, however, it splits society into an aggregate of bona fide, fully fledged consumers (a graduated quality, to be sure), and a category of failed consumers – those who are unable for various reasons, but first and foremost for lack of adequate resources, to live up to the standards which the message prompts and instigates them to match, insistently and assertively hammering itself home and in the end recycling itself into a no-questions-asked and no-exceptions-allowed obligatory commandment. The first group are pleased with their efforts and inclined to consider their high scores in the consumer tables to be a right and proper reward for their inborn or hard-won advantages in coming to grips with the intricacies of the pursuit of happiness. The second group feel humiliated, having been assigned to the category of inferior beings: at the bottom of the league table, facing or already suffering relegation. They are ashamed of their poor performance and of its plausible causes: lack or insufficiency of talent, industry and persistence – any of these inadequacies being recast now as disgraceful, demeaning, degrading and disqualifying, even if they are viewed (or because they are viewed) as avoidable and reparable vices. The victims of the competition are publicly blamed for the resulting social inequality; yet more importantly, they tend to agree with the public verdict and blame themselves – at the cost of their self-esteem and self-confidence. An insult is thereby added to the injury; the salt of reprobation is rubbed into the open wound of misery.

Condemnation of allegedly self-inflicted social inferiority has been stretched to embrace the slightest murmur of demurral on the part of the underdog, not to mention their rebellion against the injustice of inequality as such – as well as any sympathy and commiseration for the underdog on the part of the upper dog. Dissent with the state of affairs and the mode of life responsible for its continuation is no longer seen as a justified defence of the lost/stolen (though ostensibly inalienable) human rights to be respected, have their principles recognized and offered equal treatment, but, to quote Nietzsche, as 'more harmful than any vice . . . practical sympathy with all the botched and the weak',[35] and for that reason as the 'greatest danger' that 'always lay in indulgence and sufferance'[36] for them and their kind.

Such contrived public beliefs serve as a highly effective shield protecting socially produced inequality against any serious attempt, commanding wide social support, to stem its tide, and perhaps even hold back and reduce its spread. They cannot, however, prevent the rise and accumulation of wrath and rancour in those who are treated daily to the spectacle of the glittering prizes supposedly offered to every current and would-be consumer (rewards preconceived as tantamount to a life of happiness), coupled with the experience of exclusion, day in, day out, and being blackballed from the feast. Occasionally, the hoards of stocked anger explode in a short-lived orgy of destruction (as happened a couple of years ago in the Tottenham riots of failed/disqualified consumers) – expressing, however, the desperate desire of the deprived to enter the consumer paradise for at least a fleeting moment, rather than their intention to question and challenge the fundamental tenet of consumerist society: the axiom that the pursuit of happiness equals shopping and that happiness is to be sought and is waiting to be found on shop shelves.

Once supplemented by and crowned with the assent of the victims with that verdict, the ascription of guilt to the victims of inequality effectively precludes the recycling of dissent fed by humiliation into a programme for an alternative mode of a gratifying life grounded in a differently organized society. Dissent suffers the lot of most other aspects of human togetherness: it tends to be, so to speak, 'deregulated' and 'individualized'. The sentiments of injustice that could otherwise be deployed in the service of greater equality are refocused on the nearest outposts of consumerism, splintered into myriads of individual grievances resistant to aggregation and blending – and in sporadic acts of envy and vengeance targeted against other individuals within sight and reach. The scattered outbursts of wrath offer temporary release to the poisonous emotions that are normally tamed and blocked, and bring an equally short-lived respite – though only to make the placid, resigned surrender to the detested and hated injustices of daily life somewhat easier to bear. And as Richard Rorty insightfully warned a few years ago, 'If the proles can be distracted from their own despair by media-created pseudo-events . . . the super-rich will have little to fear.'[37]

All varieties of social inequality derive from the division between the haves and the have-nots, as Miguel Cervantes de Saavedra noted half a millennium ago. But in different times the having or not having of *different* objects is, respectively, the state most passionately desired and the state most passionately resented. Two centuries ago in Europe, only a few decades ago in many places distant from Europe, and up to today in quite a few battlegrounds of tribal wars or home-grown saviours' playgrounds, the prime object setting the have-nots and the haves in conflict was or continues to be bread or rice (perpetually in insufficient supply). Thanks to God, science, technology and/or certain reasonable political undertakings, this is no longer the case – which does not mean, however, that the age-old division is dead and buried. On the contrary, the objects of desire whose absence is most violently resented are nowadays many and varied – and their numbers, as well as the temptation to have them, grow by the day. And so the wrath, humiliation, spite and grudges aroused by *not* having them also grow – as well as the urge to destroy what can't be had. Looting shops and setting them on fire derive from the same source and gratify the same longing.

We are all consumers now, consumers first and foremost, consumers by right and by duty. The day after the 9/11 outrage, George W. Bush, calling on Americans to get over the trauma and go back to normal, found no better precept than to 'go back shopping'. It is the level of our shopping activity and the ease with which we dispose of one object of consumption in order to replace it with a 'new and improved' one which serves as the prime measure of our social standing and our score in the competition for life success. For all the problems we encounter on the road away from trouble and towards satisfaction we seek the solutions in shops. From cradle to coffin we are trained and drilled to treat shops as pharmacies filled with drugs to cure or at least mitigate all the illnesses and afflictions of our lives and lives in common. Shops and shopping thereby acquire a fully and truly eschatological dimension. Supermarkets, as George Ritzer famously put it, are our temples; and so, I may add, are shopping lists our breviaries, while strolls through shopping malls become our pilgrimages. Buying on impulse and getting rid of possessions that are no longer sufficiently attractive in order to put more attractive ones in their place are our most enthusing emotions. Fullness of consumer enjoyment means fullness of life. I shop, therefore I am. To shop or not to shop is no longer the question.

For defective consumers, those updated versions of have-nots, non-shopping is the jarring and festering stigma of a life unfulfilled, a mark of nonentity and good-for-nothingness. Not just of the absence of pleasure, but of the absence of human dignity. Indeed, of the absence of life's meaning. Ultimately, of humanity and any other ground for self-respect and the respect of others.

For legitimate members of the congregation, supermarkets may be temples of worship and destinations of ritual pilgrimage. For the anathemized, found faulty and so banished by the Church of Consumers, they are the outposts of the enemy, provocatively placed on the land of their exile. Heavily guarded ramparts bar access to the goods which protect others from a similar fate: as George W. Bush would have to agree, they bar a return (and for youngsters who have never yet sat on a pew, access) to 'normality'. Steel gratings and blinds, CCTV cameras, uniformed security guards at the entry and others in plainclothes hidden inside only add to the atmosphere of a battlefield and ongoing hostilities. Those armed and closely watched citadels of the 'enemy in our midst' serve as a day in, day out reminder of the natives' degradation, inferiority, misery and humiliation. Defiant in their haughty and arrogant inaccessibility, they seem to shout: I dare you! But dare you what?

The most commonly and insistently ham-
mered home answer to that last question is
'one-upmanship'. That is, trying to outdo and
outscore the next-door neighbour or workmate
in the game of inequality of social standings.
One-upmanship presumes inequality. Social
inequality is one-upmanship's natural habitat
and grazing ground – though simultaneously its
summary product. The game of one-upmanship
implies and insinuates that the way to repair the
damage perpetrated thus far by inequality is
more inequality. Its attraction rests in the promise
of turning the inequality of players from a bane
into an asset; or rather of turning the social,
jointly suffered bane of inequality into an individually enjoyed asset – by measuring one's own
success by the degree of others' failure, the extent
of one's advancement by the number of others
lagging behind, and all in all, one's rise in value
by the scope of the devaluation of others.

A few months ago François Flahault published
a remarkable study of the idea of the common
good and the realities for which it stands.[38] For
many years now that indefatigable explorer and
interpreter of the manifest and latent subtleties
of interhuman relations and exchanges has been

engaged in the struggle against the 'individualist and utilitarianist' concept of man: the explicit or covert premise of much of Western social science, assuming that *individuals precede society*, and therefore that society – the fact of human togetherness – needs to be explained by the endemic attributes of human individuals. Flahault is one of the most consistent and persistent promoters of the opposite view: that *society precedes individuals*, and for that reason the thought and actions of individuals, including the very fact of acting individually and, so to speak, 'being individuals', need to be explained as deriving from the fundamental fact of living-in-society. His book dedicated to the 'common good' weaves together the threads spun in his lifelong research; it can be seen as a summary and crowning of his life work thus far.

The major message of the new study, focused on the current shape of our radically 'individualized' society, is that the idea of human rights is currently utilized to replace and eliminate the concept of 'good politics' – whereas, to be realistic, that idea cannot but be founded on the idea of the *common* good. Human existence and coexistence combining into social life constitute the good common to us all, from which and thanks to which all cultural and social goods derive. The pursuit of happiness should for that reason focus on the promotion of experiences, institutions and other *cultural and natural realities of life-in-common* – instead of concentrating on indices of wealth, which tend to recast human togetherness as a site of individual competitiveness, rivalry and infighting.

In his review of Flahault's book,[39] Serge Audier points out that Serge Latouche's or Patrick Viveret's model of conviviality,[40] while coming close to the idea advocated by Flahault as an alternative to present-day individualism, goes back a long way – even though for most of the time it has stayed on the sparsely and rarely visited outskirts of public debate. Already in his *Physiology of Taste*, published in 1825, Brillat-Savarin insisted that 'gourmandise', the delights of 'commensality', the mirth of sitting next to each other around the table, the pleasures of sharing food, drinks, jokes and merriment, were some of the essential bonds of society. The current meaning of the idea of conviviality, as togetherness emancipated from and unmutilated by the joint forces of bureaucracy and technology, was introduced,

elaborated and fully shaped in the works of Ivan
Illich. A philosopher of Austrian origin, Roman
Catholic priest and acute social critic, he was he
author of *Tools of Conviviality* (1973), protesting
against what he called the 'war on subsistence'
waged by the 'professional elite'. Let me add,
however, that the commercial opportunities
hidden in the attractions of those models of conviviality have since been discovered and avidly
embraced by consumer markets; like so many
other social and ethical impulses, they have been
commercialized and, as a rule, stamped with
brand logos. They have also entered into GNP
statistics – their share in money changing hands
rising steadily, and thus far unstoppably . . .

The point, therefore – and a point to which
we don't as yet have a convincing and empirically
grounded answer – is whether the joys of conviviality are capable of replacing the pursuit of
riches, the enjoyment of market-supplied con-
sumables and one-upmanship, all combining
into the idea of infinite economic growth, in
their role of the well-nigh universally accepted
recipes for a happy life. To put it in a nutshell,
can our desire for the pleasures of conviviality,
however 'natural', 'endemic' and 'spontaneous'

they might be, be pursued inside the currently prevailing kind of society, by-passing the mediation of marketing and without falling therefore into the trap of utilitarianism?

Attempts are currently being made to do just that. One example is Slow Food, an international (and now coming close to the status of global) movement founded in Italy by Carlo Petrini in 1986. Promoted as an alternative to fast food, it strives to preserve traditional and regional cuisine and encourages the farming of plants, seeds and livestock characteristic of the local ecosystem. The movement has expanded planetwide, to reach over 100,000 members in 150 countries. Its goals of sustainable foods and the promotion of local small businesses are paralleled by a political agenda directed against the globalization of agricultural products. Its underlying objective, and indeed its animating idea, is the resurrection and rediscovery of the almost forgotten joys of conviviality, of togetherness and cooperation in the pursuit of shared goals as the alternative to the cruel pleasures of one-upmanship and the rat race. We can read in Wikipedia that 1,300 local *convivia* chapters presently exist: 360 of them in Italy – known as *condotte* – have

35,000 members between them. The movement is decentralized: each *convivium* has a leader who is responsible for promoting local artisans, local farmers, and local flavours through regional events such as taste workshops, wine tastings, and farmers' markets. Slow Food offices have been opened in Switzerland (1995), Germany (1998), New York City (2000), France (2003), Japan (2005), and most recently in the United Kingdom and Chile.

The Slow Food movement (followed in 1999, by the way, by the Cittaslow initiative, similar in its values and intention, which has since spread to fourteen countries) is only one example – still relatively small in scale and little more than a tentative and inchoate testing of the ground – of what can be done to try to prevent the social disaster that may befall a planet in the grip of a consumerist orgy, aided and abetted by the consumer market's conquest of the human desire of happiness – a disaster all but certain to befall us if no attempts are made to mitigate or to finish off things, and things are allowed to 'go on as usual'. If the latter happens, it would surely mean 'deepening the asymmetries, inequalities and injustices, between generations as well as countries', as Harald Welzer recently warned in his thorough study of the social consequences of ongoing, and to a large extent unavoidable, climate change, brought about in no small measure by our collective decision to pursue happiness through rising consumption.[41] The point is, though, that 'the world of global capitalism' is blatantly inadequate to undertake, let alone to see through, 'long-term purposes' of the kind which the prevention of catastrophe would require. Nothing less than a radical rethinking and revision of the way we live, and the values that guide it, will do. As Welzer writes:

> What is needed, precisely in times of crisis, is to develop visions or at least ideas that have never been thought before. They may all sound naïve, but it is not really. Besides, what could be more naïve than to imagine that the train bringing destruction on a mass scale will change its speed and course if people inside it run in the opposite direction? As Albert Einstein said, problems cannot be solved with the thought pattern that led to them originally. It is necessary to change course, and for that the train must first be brought to a halt.

And he continues:

> Individual strategies against climate change
> have a mainly sedative function. The level of
> international politics offers the prospect of
> change only in a distant future, and so cultural
> action is left with the *middle level*, the level of
> one's own society, and the democratic issue of
> how people want to live in the future . . . The
> focus would be on citizens who do not *settle*
> *for* renunciation – fewer car journeys, more
> tram rides – but contribute culturally to
> changes that they consider to be *good*.

Well – when (if) it comes to the crunch, do
not say you haven't been warned. Best of all,
though, for you as much as for me and for the
rest of us, is to stop the crunch from material-
izing when stopping it still remains within our
conjoined human capacity . . .

The 'naturalness' of social inequality

We have been trained and drilled to believe that
the well-being of the many is best promoted by
tending to, grooming and honing, supporting
and rewarding the abilities of the few. Abilities,

we believe, are unequally distributed by their nature; some people are thereby predisposed to achieve what others could never attain however hard they tried. Those blessed with abilities are few and far between, while those having no ability or only its inferior variety are many; indeed, most of us, members of the human species, belong to that latter category. This is, we are insistently told, why the hierarchy of social standings and privileges has the likeness of a pyramid: the higher the level attained, the narrower the group of people able to climb it.

Placating to pangs of conscience and ego-enhancing as they are, such beliefs are pleasing and welcome for those up the hierarchy. But as arguments that reduce frustration and self-reproof, they are also good news of sorts for all those on the lower rungs of the ladder. They also deliver a salutary warning to all those who did not heed the original message and aimed higher than their inborn ability would permit them to achieve. All in all, such news prompts us to reconcile ourselves to the eerie, uncannily swelling inequality of the points of arrival by alleviating the pain of surrender and resignation to failure, while stretching the odds against dissent and resistance. To cut a long story short, they help social inequality to persist and deepen unabated. As Daniel Dorling suggests,

> Social inequality within rich countries persists because of a continued belief in the tenets of injustice, and it can be a shock for people to realize that there might be something wrong with much of the ideological fabric of the society we live in. Just as those whose families once owned the slave plantations will have seen such ownership as natural in a time of slavery, and just as not allowing women to vote was once portrayed as 'nature's way', so too great injustices of our times are, for many, simply part of the landscape of normality.[42]

In his fundamental study of popular reactions to inequality (*Injustice: The Social Bases of Obedience and Revolt*) Barrington Moore Jr suggested that in the opposition between ideas of 'justice' and 'injustice', it is the second that is the primary, 'unmarked' notion – whereas its opposite, the notion of 'justice', tends to be defined in reference to the other.[43] In any particular social setting, the standard of justice is so to speak invoked, insinuated or even dictated by the form of injustice felt to be most obnoxious, most painful and most infuriating at the moment – and therefore most passionately desired to be overcome and eliminated; in short, 'justice' is understood as a denial of a *specific case* of 'injustice'. He also suggested that, however severe, oppressive and repellent human conditions might have been, they were seldom if ever cast as unjust – providing they were experienced and suffered long enough to gell into 'normal' or 'natural'; having never experienced more favourable conditions in which 'people like us' lived, or remembering those conditions ever more vaguely, people had nothing with which to compare their current plight and so saw no case (no justification or no realistic chance) for rebellion. It was, however, the turning of the screw a notch further, a demand, however tiny, added to the long list of harsh requisitions already confronted – in other words a relatively modest worsening of living conditions – that was instantly classified as a case of injustice calling for resistance and counteraction.

Medieval peasants, for instance, were by and large reconciled to the blatant inequality between their own and their lords' living conditions and would not object to their routinely demanded villein services and corvées, however burdensome and otiose they might currently be – but any, even tiny increase in the lords' demands and pressures could ignite a peasant uprising in defence of 'customary rights', the status quo under assault. In another instance, unionized workers in modern factories used to go on strike in reaction to a wage increase accorded to workers employed in another factory, in the same trade and with the same skills, yet denied to them – or when the wages of workers whom they considered to be placed lower in the hierarchy of skills were levelled up to their own earnings: in both cases, the 'injustice' to which they objected and which they fought back against was an unfavourable *change* in the status hierarchy they had come to consider 'normal' or 'natural', a case of *relative* deprivation.

The perception of 'injustice' calling for active resistance therefore derived from *comparison*: of one's present plight with the past conditions that had had enough time to congeal into 'normality', or one's status position with that of 'naturally the same' or 'naturally inferior' status. For most people most of the time, 'unjust' meant an adverse departure from the 'natural' (read: habitual). The 'natural' was neither just nor unjust – it was, simply, 'in the order of things', 'as the things were' and were bound to be, full stop. Resisting departure from the 'natural' meant, ultimately, defence of a familiar order.

That was at least the case in the past investigated by Barrington Moore Jr and the researchers of the phenomenon of 'relative deprivation'. No longer, though . . . Nowadays, neither 'others like us' nor our own past statuses or standards of life, are necessarily the 'natural' reference points for comparison. All forms of life, 'high' and 'low', are now on public display and so within everybody's sight – and so ostensibly, temptingly even if deceptively, in everybody's reach; or at least 'on offer' to everybody. Any form of life, however distant in space or time and however exotic, may in principle be picked out as the reference point for comparison with one's own and as a yardstick for its evaluation. All the more so because of the habit of documentaries, docudramas, gossip columns and commercials not to discriminate between addressees and to send their messages into an open space to find their own landing strips as well as their own receptive targets, a habit shared in practice if not always in theory by the idea of human rights which stoutly refuse to recognize, let alone to accept and endorse, the status differences between their assumed or intended carriers. Spotting and pinpointing 'unjust' inequalities has thereby become, for all practical intents and purposes, 'deregulated' and to a large extent 'individualized', in the sense of having been left to subjective judgement.

Individually made judgements do occasionally overlap or coalesce, yet as a result of public contention and negotiation of individual choices, rather than of a standpoint determined by class or category. The extent of consent and the social composition of the agreeing camp is shown in opinion surveys, which presume (whether correctly or counterfactually) the autonomy of respondents and the independence of their choices; one is tempted to conclude that the statistics published by pollsters are the main, perhaps even the sole, occasions for diffused and scattered opinions to congeal into 'social facts' in the Durkheimian sense. Take, for instance, the pollsters' finding that after the publication of the

results of a year-long inquiry by the British High
Pay Commission four out of five of the questioned members of the public believed the pay
and bonuses for the top executives were out of
control, while two-thirds did not trust companies to set pay and bonuses responsibly. Those
two statistical majorities obviously considered
pay and bonuses of top executives excessive,
unjust, and certainly 'unnatural'. Yet they seem
to have simultaneously endorsed the 'naturalness' of that anomaly . . . None of the statistically
composed majorities has shown any sign of
uniting in any other than a statistical sense in
their opposition to the unnatural excesses of
inequality, even though the idea that the growth
in the average pay of British top executives by
more than 4,000 per cent in the last thirty years
has been due to a similar growth in British home-
grown 'natural talents' in numbers and abilities
would most certainly defy belief even for the
most gullible in our midst.

We have seen before that over many centuries
the belief in the natural inequality of human
individual talents, abilities and capacities
remained one of the most powerful factors con-

tributing to the placid acceptance of extant social inequality; at the same time, however, it provided a moderately effective brake on a stretching of the extent of the latter – offering a benchmark from which to spot and measure 'unnatural' (read: excessive) and therefore unjust dimensions of inequality, demanding repair. At times, as in the heyday of the social ('welfare') state, it could even prompt some mitigation of the distance between the top and the bottom of the social hierarchy. Today's social inequality, it seems, finds ways to self-perpetuate without resorting to the pretence of its 'naturalness'. It seems to have gained rather than lost as a result. True, it needs to seek other arguments to rely on in defence of its legitimacy. But in exchange, having dropped the 'naturalness' argument from its plaidoyer, it has got rid of its inalienable companion, the charge of 'unnaturalness' against its excesses – or at least acquired the capacity to play it down and neutralize its effects. In addition to a capacity for self-perpetuation, it has gained a capacity to self-propagate and self-intensify. The sky is now the limit for its growth . . .

Rivalry as the key to justice

One of the founders and most distinguished writers of the pragmatist school in philosophy, Charles S. Peirce, defined 'thing' as everything we can talk and think about. In other words, it is we the humans, the *subjects*, the sentient and thinking beings, who – armed as we are with consciousness and self-awareness – bring 'things' into being by making them *objects* of our thought and talk.

Saying that, Peirce followed the path blazed by an acknowledged pioneer of modern philosophy, René Descartes, who, searching for an ultimate and unquestionable proof of existence (that is, not to be misled by some malevolent and crafty imp into believing in the existence of what in fact is but a mere figment of the imagination) settled for that very *act of searching* – prompted, as it were, by having a doubt and thinking about how to get rid of it – as all the proof one needs to be certain of existing. As there cannot be a doubt without a doubting being, or a thought without a thinking being, one's experience of doubting and thinking is indeed all the proof, necessary as well as sufficient, one needs in order to reassure oneself of one's own existence. It is by that act of doubting and thinking that we, human beings, set ourselves apart from the unthinking rest of creation.

In a nutshell, according to Descartes, we – *thinking* beings – are *subjects*. The rest of the beings are *things* – *objects* of our thought. There is therefore an essential difference and an unencroachable gap between subject and object, between the 'ego' who thinks, and the 'it' thought of or about by the ego: the first being the active, creative side in their relationship, whereas the second is doomed to remain on the receiving side of the subject's actions. Equipped with awareness, subject 'means' and 'intends' (has 'motives'); and has 'will' to act on those motives. Objects, on the contrary, lack all that. In stark opposition to subjects, objects – 'things' – are lifeless, inactive, acquiescent, apathetic, compliant, docile, suffering and enduring: they are cast firmly on the receiving side of action. 'Subject' is she or he who acts; 'object' is what is acted upon. Immanuel Kant would shift the 'active' side of the subject–object relation fully to the subject's side; things are objects of the subject's scrutiny and handling – and it is to the subject that they owe their meaning and status. Bertrand

Russell would call them 'facts' ('thing *done*', but also 'things made' – from the Latin *facere*, 'to do' but also 'to make').

Things are indeed 'done' or 'made'; or (more to the point) they are designed and fashioned, produced, shaped, given form, defined, ascribed identity and all in all invested with meaning, by the human mind: an entity or a force *external* to them. As they are devoid of consciousness and therefore of the capacity *to mean*, their *meaning* is determined by 'subjects', the thinking-intending-acting beings. Subjects are free to set the meanings of things – and they do indeed set them, in terms of their relevance or irrelevance, utility or uselessness, significance or insignificance, propriety or incongruence, and in the last account their suitability or unfitness for the subjects' intentions and purposes.

To cut a long story short, the gap between subject and object, the *thinking human* and the *thing*, is for all intents and purposes unbridgeable. The idea of that 'unbridgeability', of an irreparable opposition of statuses and incurable asymmetry of their relation, is a reflection of the common experience of power-in-action: that is, of superiority and subordination, command and obedience, freedom to act and the necessity of submission . . . The description of the subject–object relation is astonishingly similar to that of 'power', 'rule' or 'domination': the ways things are defined, classified, evaluated and treated are determined by whatever the subjects might consider its own needs to be – and modulated according to the subject's convenience. One is inclined to conclude that *things*, naturally passive, numb and dumb, are there (whenever and wherever that 'there' might be) to serve the endemically active, perceptive and judging *subjects*; things are 'things' in so far as that is the case. They are not 'things' due to their intrinsic 'thingy' qualities, but because of the relation in which they are cast to the subjects. And it is the subjects who do that casting; it is the subjects who cast their objects into the status of 'things' – and hold them in that status, barring escape. That casting into the status of things is accomplished through the denial of the object's right and capacity of discretion and choice – of voicing preferences and demanding their recognition; or by stripping them of that right and/or capacity.

It should have followed from our considerations that the issue of the mode in which entities are divided into subjects and objects is potentially contentious because of its one-sidedness; in some cases it might also become hotly contested. In the event it is contested, it is hardly ever definitely resolved. In some cases, representations of the subject/object division are no more than snapshots, recording a current and in principle eminently changeable and transient stage in the ongoing power struggle. At each moment of that struggle, the subject/object division is only a temporary settlement, an invitation to further struggle or renegotiation of the status quo rather than an ultimate end to the conflict.

The most prominent and conspicuous case, and also the most consequential for our human mode of being among such conflict-ridden situations, is that of transplanting the model of subject–object relation, derived from the experience of dealing with inanimate objects, on to the relations *between* human beings or categories of human beings (as in Aristotle's classification of slaves as 'talking tools') – and tending therefore to treat humans according to the pattern elaborated and reserved for 'things'; that is, for entities assumed *a priori* to lack consciousness, motives and will, and so neither demanding nor commanding empathy or compassion. This tendency towards a misguided and illegitimate transfer of pattern, defying logic and morality, has become widespread, however, in our liquid modern, individualized society of consumers, and continues to show every sign of gathering force.

A large, probably the major part of the responsibility for such a turn of affairs is borne by the spectacular advance of consumerist culture, which posits the totality of the inhabited world as a huge container filled to the brim with nothing else but objects of potential consumption, thereby justifying and promoting the perception, assessment and evaluation of each and every worldly entity by the standards set in the practices of consumer markets. Those standards establish starkly asymmetrical relations between clients and commodities, consumers and consumer goods: the first expecting from the second solely the gratification of their needs, desires and wants, with the second deriving their sole meaning and value from the degree to which they meet those expectations. Consumers are free to set apart the desirable from the undesirable or indifferent, insignificant or irrelevant objects – as well as free to determine to what extent the objects deemed desirable or in one or another way 'relevant' to the consumers' own needs and intentions meet their expectations, and for how long those objects retain their assumed desirability and/or relevance unimpaired.

The 'things' meant for consumption retain their utility for consumers – their one and only raison d'être – as long as their estimated capacity to give pleasure remains undiminished; and not a moment longer. One does not swear loyalty to the commodities – the 'things' – one buys in a shop: one does not promise (let alone undertake an obligation) to allow them to clutter up the living space a moment after the pleasures or comforts they offer have been exhausted. Delivering the promised pleasures or comforts is the only use of the purchased commodities; once the pleasures or comforts stop being offered and supplied, or once a chance of obtaining more satisfaction or a better quality of satisfaction elsewhere has been spotted by their owner/user, they can be, ought to be, and usually are disposed of and replaced.

It is this pattern of client–commodity or user–utility relationship which is grafted upon human-to-human interaction and drilled into us all, consumers in a society of consumers, from early childhood and throughout our lives. This drilling bears a major responsibility for the current frailty of human bonds and the fluidity of human associations and partnerships – while that brittleness and revocability of human bonds are in their turn a prolific and permanent source of the fears of exclusion, abandonment and loneliness haunting so many of us these days and causing so much spiritual anxiety and unhappiness. And no wonder: the incurably asymmetrical model of the subject–object relation, once taken over and recycled by the consumer market in the likeness of the client–commodity pattern, shows itself to be singularly unfit to guide and service a human togetherness and interaction in which we all play, simultaneously or intermittently, the subject's and object's role. Unlike the client–commodity pattern, the human–human relationship is symmetrical; both sides of the relation are 'subjects' and 'objects' at the same time, and the two aspects they assume cannot be separated from each other. Both are motivated agents, sources of initiative and composers of meanings – the scene-setting has to be two-sided because they co-author the scenario in the course of the interaction in which they are both active participants: doers and sufferers at the same time. Unless both sides of the interaction agree to play both the subject's and the object's roles, and carry the risks that are bound to follow, a truly and fully human relationship (that is, a relation requiring a genuine encounter and pre-ceding cooperation of subject and object) is inconceivable.

Risks are there, and stay there – irremovable and causing perpetual tension because of the permanently present possibility of a clash between two subjectivities: between *two autono-mous, self-propelling agents*, viewing the shared situation from separate perspectives, pursuing objectives not coordinated in advance and hardly ever fully aligned. Frictions are therefore unavoid-able, and the protagonists have no alternative but to brace themselves for the prospects of cum-bersome and often thorny and prickly negotia-tions, uncomfortable compromises and painful self-sacrifices. None of the protagonists can claim indivisible sovereignty over the situation and full command over its development; or could seri-ously hope to acquire it. These risks are the price attached to, and inseparable from the unique, wholesome pleasures which *human-friendly, cooperative togetherness* holds in store. The agreement to pay that price is the magic spell, that opens up the gate to sesame full of treasures. But it is no wonder that many people may find the price too high and paying it too heavy a burden. It is to those people that the message of the consumer markets is directed, promising to strip human relations of the discomforts and inconveniences with which they are associated (in practice, to reshape them after the pattern of the client–commodity relation). And such promises are the reason why so many of us find the offer tempting and embrace it wholeheartedly, walking willingly into the trap while blissfully unaware of the losses which the trade-off portends.

The losses are enormous, and paid in the currency of shattered nerves and dark, vague and diffuse, free-floating fears – as life inside the trap means staying permanently alert: sniffing the possibility, even the likelihood, of malevolent intentions and clandestine plotting in every stranger, passerby, neighbour or workmate. To those who have fallen into the trap the world presents itself as saturated with suspicion and bristling with suspects; every one of its residents, or almost, is guilty until proven innocent, whereas each acquittal is only temporary, until further notice, always open to appeal or instant revocation. Any coalition entered into with other humans tends to be ad hoc and supplied with a clause, specifying exit-on-demand. Commitment, not to mention a long-term commitment, tends to be ill-advised; impermanence and flexibility of association (bound to make all inter-human bonds feel uncomfortably brittle and yet more fissiparous) are insistently recommended and much in demand: for one's safety, one tends to rely more on CCTV and armed guards at the entry than on human goodwill and friendliness.

All in all, the world after falling into such a trap is inhospitable to trust and to human solidarity and friendly cooperation. That world devalues and denigrates mutual reliance and loyalty, mutual help, disinterested cooperation and friendship for its own sake. For that reason, it grows increasingly cold, foreign and uninviting; as if we were unwelcome guests in someone else's (but whose?!) enclosure, waiting for the warrant of eviction already in the post or in someone's outbox. We feel surrounded by *rivals*, competitors in the endless game of one-upmanship, a game in which holding hands tends to be all but indistinguishable from hand-cuffing and a friendly embrace is all too often confused with incarceration. Dismissing that transformation by pointing to the antiquity of the adage 'homo homini lupus est' (man is a wolf to his fellow man) is an insult to the wolves.

4 Words against deeds: an afterthought . . .

The plight described is the ultimate consequence of substituting competition and rivalry – the mode of being derived from belief in the greed-guided enrichment of the few as the royal road to the well-being of all – for the human, all-too-human longing for cohabitation resting on friendly cooperation, mutuality, sharing, recip-rocated trust, recognition and respect.

But there is no benefit in greed. No benefit to anybody and in anybody's greed. This much should be known, understood and accepted by most of us, practitioners of the art of life in our deregulated, individualized world obsessed by growth, consumption, competition and each one for himself. And it is – by many. Ask people about the values dear to them, and the odds are that many, probably most, will name equality, mutual respect, solidarity and friendship among the topmost. But look closely at their daily behaviour, their life strategy in action, and one can bet that you'll derive from what you've seen an entirely different league table of values . . . You will be astonished to find out how wide the gap is between ideals and realities, words and deeds.

Most of us, though, are not hypocrites – certainly not by choice; not if we can avoid it. Very few people, if any, would choose to live their life in a lie. Truthfulness is also a value dear to most human hearts, and most of us would prefer to live in a world in which the need, not to mention the requirement, to lie does not often arise; best of all, never. So whence the gap between words and deeds? Is it correct to conclude that words stand little chance when confronted with reality? Yet more to the point: can the gap between words and deeds be bridged? And if so, how can such a bridge be built? Out of what kind of stuff? We yearn for an answer to that query – because if our values and so also the words we use to communicate them are not a match for the

power of what we call 'reality' and are therefore
not fit for the job, why bother? Well, it is not for
nothing we use the name 'reality' to denote
things too mighty and stubborn to wish or argue
away . . .

In 1975–6 Elias Canetti collected a number of
his essays, written over twenty-six years, in a
volume called *Das Gewissen der Worte* (in English
as *The Conscience of Words*). His intention, in his
own words, was to recall, reassemble, rethink the
few (and ever fewer) 'spiritual models' remaining
from those composed and practised in bygone
times ('before entering one of the darkest eras of
human history, whose coming they failed to
note') that still – in a 'monstrous century' in
which the 'enemies of humanity' came uncannily
close to the destruction of the earth, their ultimate objective – have retained some of their
'utility' (read: their potential to inspire *and* ability
to guide action).

The volume closes with the speech on the
profession of writer delivered by Canetti in
Munich in January 1976. In it, he confronts the
question of whether, in the present world situation, 'there is something in which writers or
people hitherto thought to be writers could be

of use'. For his starting point he picks a statement made by an unknown author on 23 August
1939: 'It's over. Were I a real writer, I should've
been able to prevent the war', a statement remarkable, in his view, for two reasons.

The first: it starts from acknowledging the
hopelessness of the situation: prevention of war
is no longer on the cards – it is, after all, 'over',
no longer any chance or hope of stopping the
approaching catastrophe in its tracks, we have
reached the limit of our capacity to act; though
all this is no reason to assume that this awesome
plight could not at some point have been averted,
that ways to avert it never existed and could
never have been found and chosen. Defeat does
not mean that the chance of victory over immi-
nent catastrophe was never there – only that it
has been aborted, by ignorance and/or neglect.
Defeat does not necessarily disqualify the potency
of a 'spiritual model' (in this case, the model of
the 'real writer') – it is only the stamina and
intensity of dedication of those who claimed to
follow it that have been disqualified.

The second: the author of the unsigned statement insists that one truth which has emerged
from the defeat unscathed is that a writer is 'real'

in so far as – as much as, and no more than – her or his words make a difference between well-being and catastrophe. In its essence, one is a 'real' writer if and only if she or he acquits herself or himself of their, the writers', vocational *responsibility* for the state of the word. What makes a writer 'real' is the *impact of words on reality*; in Canetti's rendition, the 'desire to assume responsibility for everything that can be expressed in words, and to do penance for their, the words', failure'.

Putting these two reasons together, Canetti can claim his right to conclude that 'there are no writers today, but we ought to passionately desire that there were'. To act on such a desire means to go on trying to become 'realistic', however unprepossessing the prospects of success. 'In a world which one would most readily define as the blindest of worlds, the presence of people who nevertheless insist on the possibility of its change acquires supreme importance.'

Let me add that imputing responsibility for the world to oneself is a blatantly irrational act; the decision to assume it, complete with the responsibility for that decision and its consequences, is however the last chance of saving the world's logic from the blindness it incurs from its homicidal and suicidal consequences.

Having said, or read and pondered all that, one still can't chase away the hauntingly sombre and harrowing premonition that the world, purely and simply, is not hospitable to the 'real writers' described by Canetti. The world seems to be well protected not against catastrophes, but against their prophets – while the residents of that well-protected world, as long as they are not brusquely denied the right of residence, are themselves well protected against adding to the (minute and wan) numbers of prophets scattered, crying, in their respective wildernesses. As Arthur Koestler kept reminding us (in vain as it were, in vain), the contrived blindness is hereditary . . . On the eve of another catastrophe, 'In 1933 and during the next two or three years, the only people with an intimate understanding of what went on in the young Third Reich were a few thousand refugees', a distinction which condemned them to the 'always unpopular, shrill-voiced part of Cassandra'.[44] And as the same author noted a few years later, in October 1938, 'Amos, Hosea, Jeremiah, were pretty good propagandists, and yet failed to shake their people and to warn them. Cassandra's voice was said to have pierced walls, and yet the Trojan war took place.'

It seems that one needs catastrophes to happen in order to recognize and admit (retrospectively alas, only retrospectively . . .) their coming. A chilling thought, if there ever was one. Can we ever refute it? We will never know unless we try: again and again, and ever harder.

Notes

1 James B. Davies, Susanna Sandstrom, Anthony Shorrocks and Edward N. Wolff, 'The world distribution of household wealth', Discussion Paper No. 2008/03, World Institute for Development Economics Research, United Nations University, Feb. 2008.

2 Jeremy Warner, 'Scourge of inequality is getting worse and worse', *Telegraph* blog, 3 May 2011, at http://blogs.telegraph.co.uk/finance/ jeremywarner/100010097/scourge-of-inequality-is-getting-worse-and-worse/ (accessed Jan. 2013).

3 Stewart Lansey, *The Cost of Inequality* (Gibson Square Books, 2012), p. 7.

4 Ibid., p. 16.

5 See Davies et al., 'World distribution of household wealth'.

6 Claudio Gallo, 'Exit democracy, enter tele-oligar-chy', interview with Danilo Zolo, Asia Times Online, at www.atimes.com/atimes/Global_Economy/NI26Djo1.html (accessed Jan. 2013).

7 See Glen Firebaugh, *The New Geography of Global Income Inequality* (Harvard University Press, 2003).

8 See François Bourguignon, *La mondialisation de l'inégalité* (Seuil, 2012).

9 See Monique Atlan and Roger-Pol Droit, *Humain. Une enquête philosophique sur ces révolutions qui changent nos vies* (Flammarion, 2012), p. 384.

10 Studies cited in 'Explorations in social inequal-ity', at http://www.trinity.edu/mkearl/strat.html (accessed Jan. 2013).

11 Ibid.

12 Joseph E. Stiglitz, *The Price of Inequality: The Avoidable Causes and Invisible Costs of Inequality* (Norton, 2012).

13 Daniel Dorling, *Injustice: Why Social Inequality Persists* (Policy Press, 2011), p. 132.

14 Ibid., p. 141.

15 Stewart Lansley, 'Inequality: the real cause of our economic woes', 2 Aug. 2012, at http://www.

socialenterpriselive.com/section/comment/
policy/20120802/inequality-the-real-cause-our-
economic-woes (accessed Jan. 2013).

16 Richard Wilkinson and Kate Pickett, *The Spirit
    Level: Why More Equal Societies Almost Always Do
    Better* (Allen Lane 2009).

17 Bourguignon, *La mondialisation de l'inégalité*,
    pp. 72–4.

18 Dorling, *Injustice*, p. 13.

19 Ibid., p. 197.

20 Ibid., p. 24.

21 From J. M. Coetzee, *Diary of a Bad Year* (Vintage,
    2008).

22 See Robert Heilbroner, *The Worldly Philosophers*,
    7th edn (Simon & Schuster, 2008).

23 John Stuart Mill, 'Of the stationary state,' in
    *Principles of Political Economy: With Some of Their
    Applications to Social Philosophy* (J. W. Parker,
    1848), Book 4, ch. 6.

24 See Heilbroner, *Worldly Philosophers*.

25 John Maynard Keynes, 'Economic possibilities
    for our grandchildren' (1930), in John Maynard
    Keynes, *Essays in Persuasion* (Norton, 1963),
    pp. 358–73.

26 John Maynard Keynes, in 'First Annual Report
    of the Arts Council' (1945–1946).

27 Robert Skidelsky and Edward Skidelsky, *How Much Is Enough? Money and the Good Life* (Other Press, 2012).

28 As presented by LMD on 1 Nov. 2012, see http://lmd.lk/2012/11/01/economic-conundrums/ (accessed Jan. 2013).

29 See Julia Kollewe, 'Meet the world's 10 richest billionaires', *Guardian*, 9 Nov. 2012.

30 Anja Weiss, 'The future of global inequality', in Michael Heinlein, Cordula Kropp, Judith Neumer, Angelika Poferl and Regina Römhild (eds), *Futures of Modernity* (Transcript, 2012), pp. 145, 150.

31 'Executive compensation: how much is too much?', 11 Apr. 2008, at http://www.investopedia.com/articles/fundamental-analysis/08/executive-compensation.asp#ixzz2Gq2vs9ud (accessed Jan. 2013).

32 Stephen Wright, 'Outrage over "absurd" golden handshake for ousted Yard boss Sir Ian Blair', *Mail*Online, 21 Dec. 2012, at http://www.dailymail.co.uk/news/article-1084452/Outrage-absurd-golden-handshake-ousted-Yard-boss-Sir-Ian-Blair.html#ixzz2Innx7xwd (accessed Jan. 2013).

33 Lansley, *The Cost of Inequality*, p. 141.

34 Ibid., p. 149.

35 Friedrich Nietzsche, *The Antichrist*, trans. Anthony M. Ludovici (Prometheus Books, 2000), p. 4.

36 Friedrich Nietzsche, *Thus Spoke Zarathustra*, trans. R. J. Hollingdale (Penguin Classics, 2003), p. 204.

37 See Richard Rorty, *Achieving Our Country* (Harvard University Press, 1998), p. 88.

38 François Flahault, *Où est passé le bien commun?* (Mille et Une Nuits, 2011).

39 *Le Monde*, 4 Mar. 2011.

40 See Alain Caillé, Marc Humbert, Serge Latouche and Patrick Viveret, *De la convivialité. Dialogues sur la société conviviale à venir* (La Découverte, 2011).

41 See Harald Welzer, *Climate Wars: What People Will Be Killed For in the 21st Century*, trans. Patrick Camiller (Polity, 2012), pp. 174ff.

42 Dorling, *Injustice*, p. 13.

43 Barrington Moore, Jr, *Injustice: The Social Bases of Obedience and Revolt* (Random House, 1978).

44 See Arthur Koestler, *The Invisible Writing* (1954), here quoted from Vintage edition of 2005, pp. 230–5.